Classic Cars

Classic Cars

Text by
ROGER HICKS

LONGMEADOW
P R E S S

1988 Porsche 959

PORSCHE

With high-performance cars, you normally have a choice: sheer performance, or reliability and comfort. Porsche is perhaps unique in offering at least one car which compromises on neither.

For sheer, raw performance it is hard to beat the fearsome 911 Turbo, and even the 'cooking' 911SC is in the front rank for fierce acceleration, uncompromising handling, and impressive top speed. But unlike some Italian machinery, where the paint pops off in the rain and fades in the sun, and the engine requires fettling once a week to keep it in tune, both cars are almost boringly reliable. Furthermore, the interior is surprisingly spacious, and although there is the beautiful whine of that flat-six engine, you are not deafened as you are in some bright-red V12s. What is more, the whole plot is surprisingly tractable; if you want to pootle down Rodeo Drive, you can do so without indulging in the bursts of heart-stopping acceleration alternated with tyre-screeching braking which are unavoidable with some of the Porsche's competitors.

And before the 911, there was the 356; a good deal slower, perhaps, but still with that happy combination of performance (in relation to its time) and reliability – though it must be admitted that the 356 could suffer from the tin-moth, and that rust has claimed a number of these cars prematurely. The 356 was rather more spartan than the 911, too, but it still looked beautiful and went beautifully.

Then again, there was the immortal flat-12 917, capable of well over 200 mph with the appropriate gearing. This was the car which turned Le Mans into a Porsche benefit: the 917s did the winning, while the 911s cleaned up on the Index of Performance and the class awards. Some Porsche 917s were road-legal, and along with the Ford GT40 these must rate as the most amazing sports cars of all time. In its ultimate form, the turbocharged 917/30 delivered over 1100 bhp...

Of course, there are other Porsches, though devotees of the cars with horizontally-opposed oil-cooled rear engines prefer to ignore them. There was the joint venture with Volkswagen, the 914, produced as a 914/6 with the Porsche engine and as a 914/4 with the Volkswagen motor. It was not a beautiful car, but it was less of a handful to drive than the 911, especially in the wet; for obvious reasons, the 914/4 is less sought-after. About 125,000 914s were made between 1969 and 1974, when production ceased. The reason for this cessation, at least in part, was the forthcoming launch of the 924.

The 924 horrified purists. The engine was in the wrong place (at the front); it was the wrong layout (in-line four); it had the wrong sort of cooling (water); and by the standards of Porsche in 1975, it was small at 2 litres, 122 ci (the biggest flat sixes were now 2.7 litres, 165 ci) and low-powered at 125 bhp. On the other hand, it was a very fine car, and it spawned the 924 Turbo (170, then 177 bhp) and the 'homologation special' 924 Carrera GT developing 210 bhp – the same as the original 1972 Carrera 911 RS. In 1981, the VW/Audi engine was replaced with a new 163 bhp Porsche-designed 2.5 litre four, and various 'go-faster' goodies were added to create the 944, but it was preceded in 1980 by the 928, basically a V8 version of the 924. Initially in 4.5 litre (374 ci) form with 240 bhp, it was offered two years later in 4.7 litre (387 ci) 300 bhp form.

Despite all this, the 911 refused to die, and the old flat six was bored out again; the biggest displacement to date has been the 3.3 litre (201 ci) Turbo. As a result, in the mid-to-late 1980s Porsche could offer both front- and rear-engined cars, and a range of engines which embraced an in-line four, a flat six, and a V8, with and without turbochargers – a very impressive line-up.

Somehow, history seems less appropriate when talking of Porsche than of other cars. As far as purists are concerned, there have only been two road cars – the 356, originally derived from the VW Beetle (which was, of course, also designed by Ferdinand Porsche), and the 911, though both have appeared in a variety of guises. The 356 ran from 1948 to 1965, and the 911 has been in continuous production since 1963. The other road cars are all listed above. The racing history is more complicated, and even includes a Formula One car, but that is a story which is much too long to tell here.

Facing page: (top left, top) an early 356 with split windscreen; (top left, centre) the first 356; (top left, bottom) the original 356 and a more recent model; (top right) the 356 cabriolet, which ceased production in 1965 in C form, and (bottom) the 911 Turbo, a direct descendant of the 2 litre, 130 horsepower 911 of 1963, but now with a 3.3-litre engine which develops 300 horsepower. Above: the Auto-Union racing car which bristled with innovative features, such as torsion bar suspension. Left: the very first 356, the first car to bear the Porsche name, was hand-made in Gmünd, Austria in 1948. Below left and below right: versions of the 356.

The red vehicle on these pages is a very desirable Porsche 356A (manufactured between 1955 and 1959) with a detachable hard-top offered by the factory to complement the Cabriolet body form. The flat-four engine looks diminutive inside the roomy engine compartment and it is the ancillaries that capture the attention – the cooling fan and intake filters for the carburettors being apparent immediately. For its era, the 356A Hardtop was remarkably spacious and airy. Green digits on black instruments were Porsche's trademark with the 356 model, but everything about the car was thoroughly functional and hard-wearing. Opening quarterlights in the front windows were an innovation for the A version. The silver vehicle is a pristine 356C model – with a non standard rearview mirror – in Coupé form. A total of 16,674 C models were produced between 1963 and 1965, bringing total production of the 356 up to the 76,000 mark in 16 years.

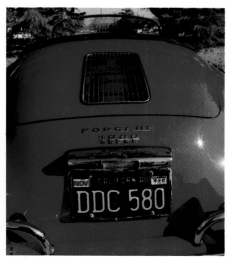

Bottom: a 356B hardtop restored to Concours standard by its American owner. Remaining pictures: a bright red 356 Speedster. The Speedster model was produced specially for the California market in America, though it was sold elsewhere in the world. It was primarily an open two-seater, though rather crude weather protection was available in the form of a black fabric hood. A total of 2,350 were made on the 356A chassis between 1955 and 1958 and are now prime collector's items. Facing page centre: the Speedster is shown beside a 911 Turbo, dubbed the Carrera Turbo in the States.

Times change but methods do not. Today, as 20 years ago when the 356 production was in full swing, the cars are pushed from one station to another on wheeled dollies in various stages of manufacture. Modern methods, however, can be seen in the new part of the works where the 928 model is assembled. The pace is quite leisurely, as accuracy and quality are far more important than speed. Power units, (top right) for the 911 and (facing page) V8s for the 928, are still hand-built and each one is dyno tested before installation.

These pages: three more examples of the 356 prepared to Concours standard. The imitation knock-on hubs on the 356A coupé (facing page top left and top right) may not be to everyone's taste but the 356B Hardtop (facing page right, lower picture) is a real beauty and the gleaming Speedster (below, left of picture) is a pristine example. The extremely high standard of preparation attained by the enthusiast is well illustrated by these fine vehicles.

A hybrid, maybe, but a production run of 125,000 in five years spells success. The VW-Porsche 914 (this page and facing page top) was produced by a company set up jointly by Volkswagen and Porsche. The 914/4 was powered by Volkswagen's four cylinder engine and the 914/6 by Porsche's 2-litre six. Facing page bottom: a sleek example of the 911 Coupé. Overleaf: a silver 911 Coupé and a chocolate brown Targa and (insets); (top left) the Porsche 928 model, (top right) a green 911 Targa, (bottom right) profile of a 928, (bottom centre) 911 Turbo 303 and (bottom left) the 911 Coupé.

Top left and top centre: the 911 Coupé. Above: a 911 Turbo. Right: a 911T, the T denoting touring trim. It was this car, which incidentally was the last normally aspirated series production Porsche (rather than having the Bosch fuel injection), which formed the basis on which the company tackled a number of sporting events with a great deal of success, notably wins in the Monte Carlo Rally in 1968, 1969 and 1970. The five-spoke, polished forged alloy wheels fitted to this car are virtually a Porsche trademark. Top right: a silky 911 Turbo. Centre right and bottom far right: two examples of the blue 911 Targa, with two different interior trims visible within the cars.

Facing page: (top left, top right and bottom right) the 3.3-litre version of the 911 Turbo which went into production in 1978; (centre) a production prototype of the 911 Turbo which had a vented grille below the rear number plate, but this did not appear in production, despite the high temperatures realised in this area by the turbocharger which spins at up to 90,000 rpm, and (bottom left) a 911. Above: a cross-section illustration of the 911, which appeared in 1963 with an air-cooled engine overslung at the rear. Left: a silver-grey 911 Turbo which first appeared with a 3 litre engine, though this was later changed to a 3.3. Below and below left: the 911 Turbo prototype.

Cross-sections of (below) the 928, which was announced in 1978, and (bottom) the 924; both have engines at the front and transmissions at the rear in transaxle form to achieve equal weight distribution at the front and back, thus giving them excellent roadholding. Remaining pictures: a selection of 911 models with a variety of trim, colour and style, including the 911SC model (facing page top). Impact-absorbing bumpers have been available for the 911 since 1973 – and standard in the UK – together with electrically-operated sunroofs and other luxury items.

Facing page centre: a 944. Below: a Targa. One Californian couldn't make up his mind whether he preferred black or Minerva blue, so he had both (remaining pictures). These 3.3-litre Turbos have non-standard BBS wheels and the blue car has a smart-looking customised interior. Both cars can reach the Californian speed limit of 55mph in around five seconds, but its the way you do it that really counts. Imports of the Turbo model into the USA virtually ceased in 1980 due to new emission rules coming into force, but the model remains much sought after.

Top: the powerful 944, which is based on the chassis of the 924 Carrera GT and uses the same front engine/rear transaxle layout. Above and facing page centre and bottom right: a customised 924 with BBS wheels, flared wheel arches and warm air extractors. Right and above right: a Turbo version of the 924, a model which broke entirely new ground for the company, giving it a far larger market than it had previously enjoyed. Facing page: (top left and top right) a 924 Turbo, which can deliver 177bhp from its 2-litre engine and (bottom left) a gleaming 924.

Top left, bottom left and above: a USA specification 911 Targa with the heavy, but practical, bumper protection insisted on by that market. Top right: the magnificent 928S. Centre right and centre left: an American-style 924 Turbo. Above left: the 928 and 928S, which cater for the company's wealthier clientèle while the 911 Targa (left) remains as popular as ever. Centre: the classic 924.

Racing Porsches. Facing page: (top and centre left) a 904; (centre right and bottom right upper picture) two cars from Porsche's brief foray into single-seat racing between 1958 and 1962; (bottom left) the 908 and (bottom right lower picture) the 904 of 1964. Above: the spaceframe 906 model designed primarily for private owners, though also used effectively by the factory on occasion. Left: the 718/2 Formula 2 of 1960 together with the 356B Carrera Abarth and the 718/RS60. Below: the Coupé and Spyder models of the 908. Bottom: a 908 fitted with a 2.1-litre, turbocharged engine.

Left: a 936 Spyder and 935 Coupé, both of which used the turbocharged 911 engine to win World Championships in 1976 and 1977. Above: a Porsche which never raced due to a change in the rules. Below left: the 935 in 1977 guise with (below right) the Kremer-bodied version. Facing page: (bottom) a 935K3 and (top) a 924 Carrera GT. Bottom: a 911 on the East African Safari.

Above and overleaf top right: the German privateer Georg Loos in his 917/10 at Nurburgring. Right: the 936 in its prototype matt black finish. Far right, top to bottom: Mark Donohue's Can-Am championship 917/30; a racing 911; the 1976 Le Mans-winning 936 and the first turbocharged 911, a racing car which came second at Le Mans in 1974 and accelerated development of the production model. Overleaf: (top left) the 911 Cabriolet of 1982; (bottom left) a 904 and a customised 911 Turbo and (bottom right) Bob Garretson's 1981 World Driver Championship 935. The 935 won world championships from 1976 to 1979 and Le Mans in 1979.

In 1965 Ford came out with the Mustang, a sports car at a reasonable price, and it was an immediate success. In 1966, when the convertible shown here was produced, more than 600,000 vehicles were sold. The seemingly endless option list allowed customers virtually to create their own car, a feature which no doubt added to the appeal of the Mustang.

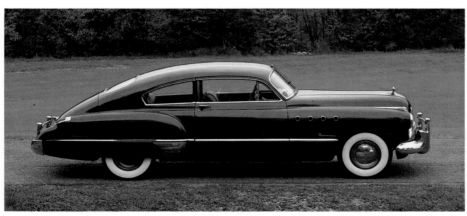

The Sedanet or Fastback styling theme had been used by Buick since 1941 and nowhere was it more attractive than on the 1949 Roadmaster Sedanet Model 76-S. The portholes on the front fenders were new, a styling gimmick that has remained a Buick trademark to this day. Note the massive over-riders on the front bumper; this was an optional feature probably designed for aggresive parking!

The breathtaking 1963 Riviera Sport Coupé was Buick's entry into the Thunderbird-dominated 'personal luxury' car market. Its razor-edged design was unlike anything else produced by GM, possessing an elegance and poise that set it apart from the rest. The Riviera was pure artistry on wheels, thanks to the gifted William L. Mitchell, who blended a subtle mix of European and American influences to create a true classic.

Facing page: an immaculate Chrysler 300 convertible dating from 1966. Arguably the first 'personal luxury' car was the Chrysler Town & Country (left and bottom right). Below left, below right and bottom left: the Chevrolet Nomad of 1957.

Chevrolet produced 1,713,478 units for the 1955 model year, 773,238 of them Bel Airs (above center). The all-new styling and the first Chevrolet V8 engine since 1917 made it popular then and a collector's item today. Minor trim changes and a full width grille distinguish the 1956 model Bel Air (above top and right) from the previous year's model. Above: a 1964 Corvair Monza Spyder convertible, the last year in which this car was produced with the original body styling.

The Billie Jo Spears song, *'57 Chevrolet* is a loving tribute to one of the best Chevrolets ever made. Its durability can be attested by its extraodinarily high survival rate, one of the many 57s still in existence is this fine example in two-toned blue and white. An option on the '57 was the famous 283 cid V8 rated at 283 hp, or one horsepower per cubic inch.

Bill Mitchell designed it, Zora Arkus Duntov engineered it and the result was the 1963 Corvette Stingray shown here. The semi boat-tail rear, novel split rear window design and pivoting, hidden headlights caused a sensation in motoring circles throughout the world. Offered as a coupé and convertible, the car was an instant success to the tune of 21,000 produced.

Not everything that came out of
Detroit in the '50s was trimmed to
excess. In fact the crème de la
crème of Chrysler's 1955 crop, the
C-300 (these pages) had
extremely clean lines. This
beautiful car, styled by Virgil
Exner, had a New Yorker body and
an Imperial grille, but the effect
was striking. The C-300 was a
grand tourer in every sense of the
word and became the first car to
hold the NASCAR, AAA and
Daytona Speedworks
championships at the same time.

Two years after Chrysler Corporation's 'Suddenly its 1960' look, Virgil Exner's finny styling was beginning to pall with the addition of hastily contrived trim and disorientated grilles, as in the case of this 1959 De Soto FireFlite convertible. This was unfortunate as the car had fine handling with power to match. More unfortunate was De Soto's position, sandwiched between the popular Dodge and Chrysler models. By 1961 poor sales had driven De Soto to extinction.

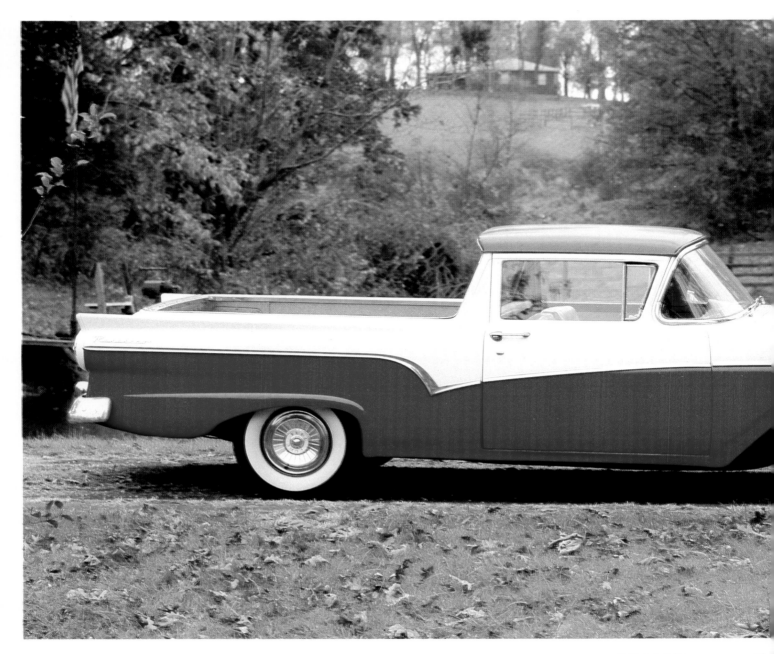

Right and far right center: the hapless Ford Edsel, which first appeared in 1958 to boost the company's sales in the mid-price range. Despite ten years of research and an intense market survey, both of which augured well, the Edsel failed and within three years it was no more. Shown here is a 1959 Ranger model. Remaining pictures: the rather more successful 1957 Ranchero half-ton pickup from Ford. Pickups had been around for years, but had resembled small trucks. The Ranchero combined the comfort of a car with the versatility of the truck and was the first of a new type of vehicle.

Launched in 1961, the new Lincoln Continental (these pages) was as different from its over-ornate predecessor as chalk is from cheese. It was also unique in many ways, being the only four door convertible available anywhere with the doors opening from the center. Tooling forward of the cowl was shared with the Thunderbird to cut costs, though few could tell.

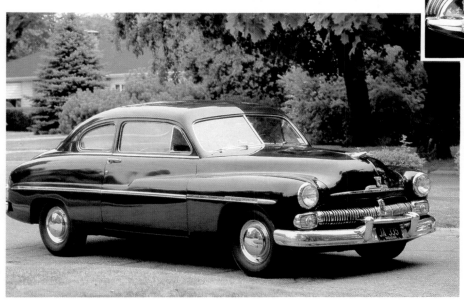

If ever there was a car which spoke for the '50s youth then it has to be the 1949-1951 Mercury. Its high waistline, rounded curves and narrow glass area begged customising and its 255.4 cid L-head V8 had enough power for cruising down the boulevard on hot summer nights. More often than not, customisers dispensed with the sliced sausage grille for something wilder and chopped the low roofline even lower. Shown here is a 1950 Mercury.

Left, top and above center: the husky 1967 Pontiac GTO, one of the fastest cars of the decade. With a 400 cubic inch V8 engine the '67 GTO could reach 60 mph from rest in 4.9 seconds and complete the standing quarter in 13.09 seconds, reaching 106.5 mph. Above: the Pontiac Le Mans Sport Coupé of 1967, the family version of the GTO.

Two Studebakers, three years apart, feature on these pages. The black car is the 1953 model designed by Robert E. Bourke, chief of Loewy's Design Studio. This is a Commander State Regal Hardtop and is powered by Studebaker's 259 cid V8. The gold and white model is the 1956 Golden Hawk. It was the same body as the '53 but heavily facelifted with the inclusion of a new hood, small, classic style grille and rudimentary fins. Under the bonnet sat the big 352 cubic inch Packard engine.

Left and above: the Tucker, possibly the most advanced car of 1948, incorporated a whole host of revolutionary and advanced features, together with superb mechanics. Only 50 were produced before the project ended in the courts. Top and inset: a 1949 Jeepster, a sporty family version of the wartime jeep produced by Willys. Above center: the first Lincoln Continental, which appeared in 1940.

▲ Mercedes SL ▼ Mercedes 260

MERCEDES

With most of the *grandes marques*, one addresses oneself to a limited range of vehicles: out-and-out sports cars, luxury cars, or perhaps sports roadsters and saloons. But Mercedes-Benz have made all of these and more, from Formula One cars to trucks, fire-engines, and ambulances. Where to begin?

One obvious place would be with the massive Benz racers from the first decade of the century, culminating in the incredible 4-cylinder 200 hp racer with a displacement of no less than 21.5 litres, 1312 ci. These chain-driven monsters were the epitome of pre-Great War racing, when brute force was all.

Another starting-point might be the S-series of supercharged straight-sixes in the 1920s and 1930s. The type numbers by which these were known are unusually informative, in that they give first the fiscal or nominal horsepower, then the actual horsepower, and finally the actual horsepower *mit Kompressor* (supercharged). Thus they began in 1927 with the 6.8 litre (415 ci) 26/120/180, otherwise known as the Sport, which delivered 120 hp unblown and 180 hp blown – the supercharger was not engaged constantly, but was only used for maximum acceleration or speed. They then progressed to a 7.1 litre (433 ci) 27/140/200 Super Sport (SS), after which they shortened the chassis by a foot and a half (50 cm) and upped the power to 27/170/225 to get the Super Sport Kurz (SSK; 'kurz' = short). Not content with that, they lightened the whole thing, race-modified the engine, and produced the 27/170/300 Super Sport Kurz Leicht (SSKL; 'leicht' = light).

After the S-series came the K-series, also superchaarged, but this time straight-eights instead of sixes. By this time, they had dropped the fiscal horsepower figures, and just quoted them with and without blower. The 1934 500K was a 5-litre (305 ci) delivering 100/160 bhp, and the 1936 540K was predictably a 5.4 litre (329 ci) and delivered 115/180 bhp. But unlike, say Rolls-Royce, Mercedes also supercharged their luxury cars; the straight-eight 'Grosser Mercedes' models boasted 7.7 litres (469 ci) and a power rating which rose from 30/150/200 in 1930 to 155/230 in 1938. Rolls-Royces were quiet; (British) Daimlers were quieter; and the sound of a 7.7 litre Mercedes when the *Kompressor* cut in has been likened to the sound of a pig being slaughtered under a railway bridge.

Or again: in 1954 there was the famous Mercedes 300SL, with a 3-litre straight six in the original roadgoing 'Gull Wing'. The 300SLR racing derivative had a 3-litre straight-eight derived from the Grand Prix engines, and a top speed in excess of 150 mph with the right final drive – though the SSKL had been clocked at 156 mph nearly a quarter of a century earlier!

And yet, alongside all this ultra-dramatic machinery, there was a steady diet of mundane four-cylinder saloons. One was the Ferdinand Porsche-designed rear-engined 1300cc (79 ci) 130 H of 1933, delivering a resounding 26 hp (gross), which is remarkable chiefly for the way in which it foreshadowed the Volkswagen and (it is said) for its downright terrifying handling. Another, and perhaps the best-known, was the extremely worthy and well-made 170 series of 1700cc (104 ci) front-engined cars, made from 1935 until well after the war.

Since the war, their bread and butter models have been climbing steadily up-market, however; although the original 180 of 1953 was a side-valve in-line four, they introduced the 300-series of 3-litre (183 ci) straight-sixes in 1951, and they have steadily been extracting more and more power from them, despite reducing the actual displacement in many cases. They returned their more expensive road-going cars to the 8-cylinder fold in the 1960s, this time with a V8 rather than a straight-eight; their earlier post-war *Grosser* models used the six, while later ones used the V8, which has also found its way into many other models, including the 'Q-car' 300EL V8 6.3. Since 1955 they have also made a line of very attractive small sports cars, beginning with the pretty but not terribly fast 190SL and now including some remarkably quick V8s.

Even now, a Mercedes-Benz cannot really be compared with a Rolls-Royce. Even the most expensive models are disappointingly spartan in their basic trim, though many extras are available to make them comparable in every way with (say) a Jaguar, probably one of their nearest competitors. Where they do score is on engineering excellence; when you drive a Mercedes-Benz, you have the feeling that everything, from the engine and transmission to the door-locks, from the unitary body to the instrument fascia, has been designed and built *properly*.

Above: the 1886 Benz three-wheeler, generally considered the world's first practical motor vehicle. Right: the wooden-framed motorcycle of 1885, which was Daimler's first vehicle. Below: the Benz 'Mylord' Coupé of 1896-99 which could reach 40 km/h. Facing page: (top) a magnificent 1908 Mercedes Edwardian tourer, with gleaming brass fittings and a dog mascot on the radiator, and (bottom) a Mercedes Simplex of 1903 with a large, limousine body.

Facing page: (top left) Daimler's first car of 1886, a converted horse-carriage; (center left) a huge 1910 limousine; (top right) the 170V of 1935; (center right) the all-conquering 1914 Grand Prix car, whose 4.5 litre engine developed 115 horsepower and won the French Grand Prix in front of a highly partisan crowd, and (bottom) the 1928 Nurnburg 460 model. Top: the 24/100/140 sportscar which had a six-cylinder, 6.2 litre engine. Above: the 320 model of 1937. Left: a short wheel-base Benz Spyder of 1902 which, although sporty in appearance, was powered by a small, 15 horsepower engine.

Top and above left: two versions of the Grand Prix car of 1914, the engine of which had four valves and three plugs per cylinder and a single overhead camshaft. Above right: Stirling Moss in thoughtful mood as mechanics work on his car. Left: the 1954 W196 streamliner, which produced 290 bhp from its eight-cylinder engine. Facing page: (top) the W25 of 1934, which was designed in record time by Hans Nibel thanks to government help; (center left) the 170S cabriolet of 1949, which re-established the reputation of Mercedes as a quality car manufacturer after the war; (center right) as an open wheel car, the 2.5 litre 1954/55 W196 became popular with drivers and proved successful for Fangio in the 1954 season, and (bottom) the W154/M of 1939, which produced 483 bhp at 7,500 rpm.

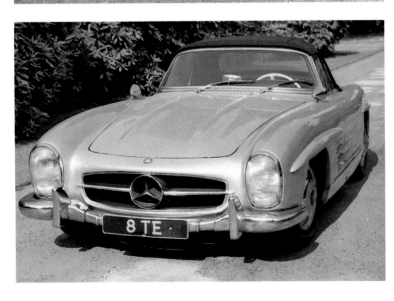

Right: the sleek sophistication of a 250C. Below: a 1968, 6.3 litre 300 SEL Facing page: (top) the modern 380SEL; (centre left) wind tunnel tests are carried out on prototype models to determine the most efficient shape; (bottom left) stylists work on scale models of possible new designs as well as a full-sized version in the background; (centre right) the factory at Gaggenau and (bottom right) the 300SEL, introduced in 1969. Overleaf: the Daimler-Benz motor museum: (inset top left) a 500K supercharged roadster; (inset bottom left) an SSK; (inset top right) a 1934-36 type 500K special roadster and (bottom right) a 1936-39 supercharged 540K.

Above: a 280SL. Below centre left: a comparison of aerodynamics. Remaining pictures: the 170S cabriolet, which developed from the saloon model. The 170 was made in 1935 and again in almost indistinguishable form in 1949-52. The standard post-war models were the saloon, convertible and convertible saloon or cabriolet.

Facing page top: the flagship of the sporting range, the 500SL, which can be identified by the rear spoiler. This model has a 4.9 litre V8 engine with fuel injection and a single overhead camshaft. Facing page bottom: the drophead 350SL Top and above left: the 380SL's engine is a scaled down version of the V8 used in the 500. These cars are the third generation of a model that first appeared in the 1960s, having been greatly improved in terms of ride, handling, performance and economy. Auto 2,000 was the title given to a project sponsored by the German Ministry of Technology. The Daimler-Benz version (above, left and facing page centre) was aimed at the long-distance touring car.

Facing page: (top left) the four-cylinder, 2.3 litre fuel-injected 230E; (top right) an attractive publicity shot of the 4.5 litre V8 450SEL; (centre left) a 250 saloon gets to grips with the snow; (centre) the diesel-powered 200D; (bottom left) the drophead 500SL, which uses the 5 litre alloy V8 engine, and (bottom right) the drophead 350SL, older brother to the 500, has a 3.5 litre V8 unit that produces 195 bhp. No doubt spurred on by the various estate car conversions to their vehicles, Mercedes introduced the T-car (left). Remaining pictures this page: the Gelandewagen, or G-car, marked Mercedes' entry into the growing cross-country vehicle market.

Mercedes-Benz Geländewagen
4x4 Station Wagen Radstand 2400 mm

Top: as with many modern sporting models, the bonnet-top badge of the SEC is absent. Above: the sleek good looks of the 500SLC. Right: the 280S. Far right: the 480SE, powered by an eight-cylinder engine capable of producing 206 bhp. Facing page: (top) the 380SEC; (centre left) the fast 280S; (centre above right) a 1978 350SLC and (centre below right) the 200, for long the basic workhorse of the Mercedes range.

▲ Jaguar Sport XJR-S 6.0   ▼ Jaguar Sport XJR 4.0

JAGUAR

'Grace, pace, space'. So ran the most famous Jaguar advertising slogan of all time, and while it is true that the three qualitites have been present in widely varying proportions in the different models, it is also indisputable that they have in most cases been combined in a particularly satisfying way.

Grace, the first of the trilogy, has been embodied in many Jaguars. The SS100 exemplifies the sports cars of the 1930s: a long, louvred bonnet, wire wheels with huge drum brakes, Lucas P100 lamps, cutaway doors, and a rear-mounted spare wheel. For decades afterwards, it inspired copyists, from truly awful Volkswagen-based horrors to the rather lovely Panther J72. Next, the XK-series sports cars exemplified the best styling of the 1950s, though they did get bigger and fatter as they progressed from the XK120 through the XK140 to the XK150; and if you wanted a really graceful saloon, there were the Mk I and Mk II 'baby Jaguars'. In 1961, the E-type took over from the XK150, and seven years later the XJ6 replaced all the other Jaguar saloons. At the time of writing, the last Jaguar to have been introduced was the XJ-S, a startlingly quick motor-car with very individual lines and the most remarkable standards of comfort. There had, however, been rumours of an impending new 'baby Jaguar' saloon for some time. In most cases, pace has been taken for granted. Some of the pre-war saloons may not have been all that fast, at least by modern standards, but the SS100 won races and even sports-car Grands Prix, and all post-war Jaguars with the exception of the pushrod-engined Mk V have been able to top 100 mph, sometimes by 50% or more. In large part, this is due to the 6-cylinder DOHC XK engine, introduced in 1949. It is an astonishingly powerful yet simple unit which has been made in capacities of 2.4, 2.8, 3.4, 3.8 and 4.2 litres (146 ci to 256 ci) with power outputs ranging from 112 bhp (1955 2.4) to 265 bhp (late 4.2 E-types) in road-going form. Since 1971, there has also been a 5.3 litre (323 ci) V-12. In production form it has one cam per bank of cylinders, and propels the manual XJ-S to well over 150 mph; it even hauls the XJ12 saloon (the V12 version of the XJ6) to something approaching the same figure. And these are only the road-going cars: when you consider such legends as the C-type and D-type racers, or the mid-engined 4-cam V12 XJ13, grace and pace were combined to an unbelievable extent, albeit at the expense of space.

Space has in any case always been a more variable commodity. The original SS100 was not a roomy car, and the pre-war saloons were mostly quite modest, but many post-war saloons have been as spacious as anyone could reasonably wish. The 1948 Mk V, the 'Wardour Street Rolls', was big, ostentatious, and no slouch; the 3.5 litre pushrod engine could take it to 91 mph. The Mk VII was a little more rounded than the MkV, and a little less dignified, but with the XK-series engine it could top 100 mph. The Mk VIII was a Mk VII with detail changes to the body, including a one-piece windscreen, and the Mk IX was a mechanically improved Mk VIII. The ultimate big saloon was the Mk X, later known as the 420, which was nearly seventeen feet long, well over six feet wide, and gave limousine comfort combined with 105 mph performance. The 'baby' Jaguars, introduced in 1955, are generally known generically as the Mk I (before 1959, with the thicker window-frames and roof-pillars) and Mk II, but they are correctly known first by their engine capacities in litres (2.4, 3.4 and 3.8) and then later as the 240 and 340; there was never a 380, though there was a 3.8S. Although very comfortable, and roomy for their overall size, they could not compete with the bigger Jaguar saloons in the space stakes. Since 1968, the XJ6 has of course been the Jaguar for space, and although no one would call it a limousine, its spaciousness is attested by the number that are used by major companies and indeed by the British government as official cars. Lastly, although rear accommodation in the XJ-S is limited, it is a genuine four-seater rather than a 2+2, and the amount of room for the driver and front-seat passenger is as generous as the luxury in which they are cosseted.

These pages: a 1937 SS 100 two-seater open sports car, which was fitted with a 2.5 straight-six using the Weslake-designed head. The car's body remained traditional, consisting of an aluminium skin over an ash frame.

Conventionally styled and outwardly similar to the SS 90, the SS 100 (these pages) was in effect William Lyons' first true production sports car. With its elegant, sweeping lines, excellent handling and lively performance, the car attracted considerable Press interest. In standard road-trim the new car was capable of around 95 mph and a 0-60 time of 12.8 seconds. Not only was the Jaguar a superb performer on the roads, it was soon to prove its worth in international competitions.

Below: a roadster XK140. Remaining pictures: the legendary XK120, which appeared in 1948 as an open two seater, but later became available in both drophead and fixed head coupé forms. William Lyons is reputed to have designed its classic body shape in less than two weeks. The fixed head variant boasted the more luxurious interior appointments of the saloons; wider doors and a roofline which was fractionally higher than that of the drophead. Although this led to an increase in weight, the FHC suffered little in terms of performance – it was still capable of 120 mph and had a 0-60 time of 9.9 seconds.

The long-awaited Mark VII saloon (these pages), with its race-proved engine, thoroughly tested chassis and torsion bar suspension, and new servo assisted brakes, was launched at the London Motor Show in October 1950. Dressed in its spectacular, flowing bodywork, which had been designed by Lyons and built by the Pressed Steel Company, the car was the sensation of the show and, at a price of under £1,000, was in a class of its own.

After four years of faithful service, the Mark VII was given a face-lift and appeared, in September 1954, as the Mark VII M (these pages). Together with bodywork changes, the engine output was raised from 160 to 190 bhp, and the gearbox ratios were made closer. The alterations resulted in increased top speed and improved fuel consumption.

Far left: the XK140 fixed-head coupé was relatively roomy compared to its XK120 predecessor. In 1956 the Mark VII M (bottom and far left inset) was replaced by the short-lived Model VIII (below) which had a one-piece windscreen and minor trim changes together with a new cylinder head which boosted performance.

Largely of monocoque-type construction, the D-type Jaguar (these pages) was a further development of the C-type. The lighter body helped the cars achieve notable victories, including the first four places in the 1957 Le Mans. Later models, such as the yellow vehicle seen here, had a stabilising fin behind the driver.

With the exception of the XJ6, the Mark II, which was available in three engine options, was the company's most successful saloon, both in terms of numbers produced and competition victories. Right, above and top left: a 3.4 litre Mark II from 1963. Far right: the XK150S which, with its 3.8 litre engine, is generally considered the finest car of the XK sports line. Top centre: a white XK150, launched in 1957 and noticeably different from earlier models.

Looking remarkably similar to the D-type, whose monocoque construction it had inherited, the magnificent E-type (these pages) was unveiled at the Geneva Motor Show in 1961. The 3.8 litre engine and gearbox were basically those used in the XK150S, but here was a car with an up-to-the-minute shape that was capable of a staggering 150 mph. Illustrated is a 1962 Series 1 fixed-head coupé.

Far right: the 2.4 litre Mark II was powered by a straight six XK engine, which was designed more for economy than speed. Though it had a top speed of 93 mph, true enthusiasts expected something more and tended to favour the larger engines, particularly the 3.8 which could cut the 2.4's 0-60 time of 17.5 seconds in half. Remaining pictures: an S type of 1963. Powered by either a 3.4 or 3.8 litre engine, the S type was designed to complement the existing Mark II and Mark X.

Now over 20 years old, the E-type is still a stunning 'good looker' with performance to match. When it appeared, however, its impact can well be imagined. What amazed the *cognoscenti* even more than its pace was its superb handling and road-holding, due in no small part to the completely new independent rear suspension designed by Heynes. Right, below right and facing page: a 4.2 litre Series 1 roadster from 1965 and (remaining pictures) a fixed head model. The new, larger engine was accompanied by an improved gearbox, clutch and exhaust, together with new seats.

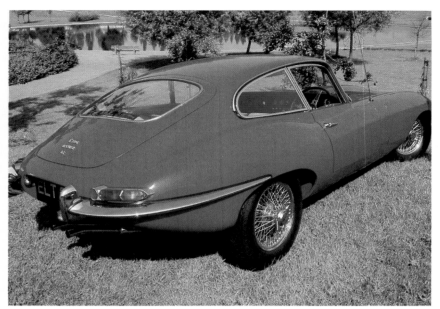

Left and bottom left: a fixed-head E-type of 1965. Remaining pictures: a smart 3.4 litre S type of 1966. Among the less obvious differences between the Mark II and the S type were slim-line bumpers, differently positioned sidelights and indicators and re-shaped rear wheel arches. Rear suspension followed the pattern set by the Mark X, this being an independent coil spring and damper arrangement rather than the Mark II's leaf springs. Internally the S type featured some of the luxury of the Mark X.

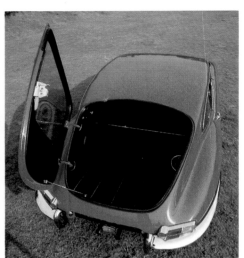

These pages and overleaf: the 1966 2+2 E-type, which added a degree of practicality to the car's undoubted panache. Apart from the vehicle's extended wheelbase, the height was increased by 2 inches and the doors were widened considerably to allow access to the rear seats. Mechanical changes on the new car were minimal, but automatic transmission now became an option. A weight increase of 2.5 cwt took its toll on performance, but the vehicle could still reach 60 mph in less than 9 seconds.

Generally considered to be the most significant model ever produced by Jaguar, the XJ6, which appeared in 1968, was to become part of the rationalisation plan that witnessed the gradual demise of all other saloon models. The car had been four years in the making and demand soon far outstripped production. These pages: a 4.2 litre 1972 model that, with the introduction of updated versions, later became known as the Series I.

These pages: the famous lightweight E-type that was raced by the German duo of Peter Lindner and Peter Nocker. Only 12 of these special, aluminium-bodied competition machines were ever built. Powered by a fuel injected 3.8 litre engine which made use of an aluminium block and could deliver 344 bhp, the car was fitted with a five speed ZF gearbox. Top speed of this much modified car, with its aerodynamically designed rear, was in the region of 170mph.

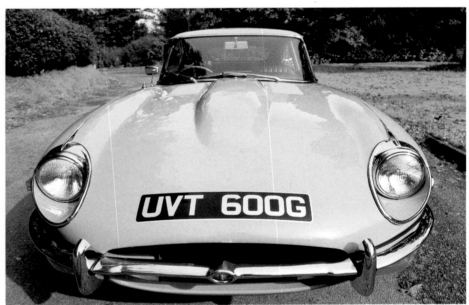

The 2+2 E-type (these pages) shared the improvements made to the remainder of the line with the introduction of the Series 2. Additionally, however, the angle of the windscreen was altered by bringing its base further forward and thus improving the car's appearance. Wire wheels were retained as a standard on all E-types until the introduction of wider tyres on the Series 3 in 1971.

In 1966 the Mark II was put through an economising process which included plastic taking over from leather for the seats. The following year further changes were made and the Mark II disappeared, to be replaced by the 240 and 340 models. The 340 (left and below) was dropped from the range on the appearance of the XJ6, but the 240 (centre left and bottom left) remained. Bottom right and far left: the luxurious 420G which first appeared in 1966 as a replacement for the Mark X, which it greatly resembled.

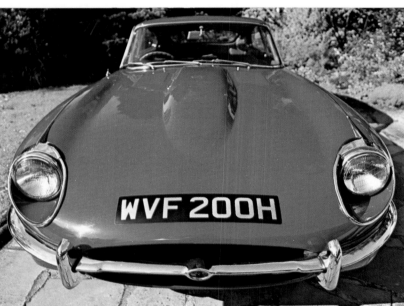

Originally intended as an option, the 4.2 engine soon became standard on the E-type, as evidenced (below). These pages and overleaf: the open two-seater which could be used with its hard top either fitted or removed. Among the Series 2's modifications over its predecessor were: an enlarged air intake, new side/indicator light cluster and the open headlights which had appeared a little earlier. Triple wipers remained for the time being.

Right: one of the last E-types to be produced: a 1975 Series 3 roadster. The fixed-head coupé had disappeared in 1970 and the 2+2 was dropped in 1973. Increased demands on the E-type's 4.2 litre engine made by the American anti-pollution laws hastened the introduction of an all new V12 engine. Capacity of the aluminium unit was 5.3 litres. This exciting addition to the Jaguar range was unveiled in 1971 in the considerably altered Series 3, which is readily identifiable by the air intake grille. Below and bottom left: a Series 3 roadster.

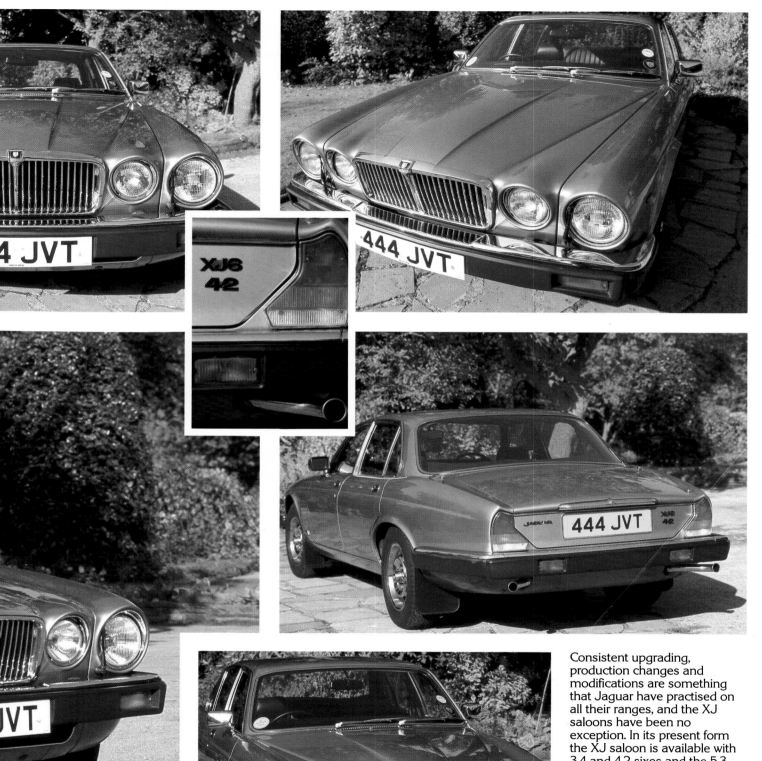

Consistent upgrading, production changes and modifications are something that Jaguar have practised on all their ranges, and the XJ saloons have been no exception. In its present form the XJ saloon is available with 3.4 and 4.2 sixes and the 5.3 litre V12. The 2.8 option was dropped in 1973. The long wheelbase variant was introduced in 1972 as the XJ6 L, and has since become standard. Shown here is a Series 3 4.2 litre XJ6 with new-style radiator grille, rear light cluster, door handles, bumpers and wheels.

Shown (these pages) is an independent but nonetheless stylish estate car modification based on the superb XJS HE. Converted by Lynx Engineering and dubbed the Eventer, the car's advertising literature claims a combination of 'extra space with amazing grace and thrilling pace'. There can be little doubt that for the motorist who requires estate car capacity and sports car performance, the Eventer offers the ultimate solution.

The XJS was introduced in 1975 as a direct replacement for the E-type. A hard top design was decided on because of legislation which at the time was expected to affect the American market. Though the car's shape met wih a mixed reaction there can be no doubt that the XJS, with performance equal to the E-type and comfort on a par with the saloons, is in the best traditions of the marque. Above, bottom and left: the standard XJS HE and (below) a Lynx Engineering Spyder conversion.

Below: the Lynx Engineering Spyder conversion of the XJS. The high efficiency HE engine, developed in conjunction with an outside team, now features on all the latest 5.3 litre V12 cars (these pages). This Series 3 XJ12 sports re-designed wheel rims and a Jaguar-fitted electric sunroof.

Top left: a GTO, much sought after by enthusiasts. Left: the cycle-winged 166 Spyder Corsa. Above: the 330GT 2+2 V12, which was never very popular due to its rather ordinary looks. Below: the 1954 860 Monza, a real brute to drive. Facing page: two views of David Piper's 1965 365P2/3 chassis No. 0836.

Facing page: (top) a 250GT berlinetta, called the Tour de France, in production from 1955 to 1959; (remaining pictures) the 206SP, perhaps the sleekest and most beautiful Ferrari ever. Top left: the 4.4 litre engine of the Lampredi designed twin overhead camshaft six cylinder 121LM. Above and bottom centre: the elegant 330GTC. Left: the 365GT 2+2. Below: a Dino 246GT. Bottom left and bottom right: one of only three 250LMBs ever built.

Facing page: two fine 275GTB/4s as restored in America. Top and centre left: a 250GTO, one of a production run of 39. Centre right: a 365GT 2+2. Left: the Dino 246GT, which was relatively inexpensive when it first appeared. Above: a beautiful 1953 340MM, chassis No. 0350, which has been restored to its original two-tone colour scheme by David Cottingham.

Left and below: one of the oldest Ferraris in existence, a 166MM Superleggera Touring Spyder with chassis No. C0161. Owned by former USA race driver Briggs Cunningham, the car now resides in his museum in California. Above: the Rocchi-designed V12 330P4. Above left: a 365 P2/3. Facing page top: a 512M in S specification. The car has been owned and raced by a number of British drivers and is now fully restored to concours condition. Facing page bottom: a 1953 340MM which is stilled raced occasionally.

Previous pages: Niki Lauda at Monaco in the 1974 312B3. Left: Lauda in the 1974 Brazilian Grand Prix. Below left: Clay Regazzoni (left) and Niki Lauda after a pre-race briefing. Below: Lauda in the 1975 312T. Bottom: Lauda in the 1974 British Grand Prix at Brands Hatch in which he led for 73 of the 75 laps. Facing page: (top) and (overleaf) Gilles Villeneuve in the turbo-charged 126C V6 1.5 litre car at the 1981 Monaco GP and (bottom) Lauda in the 1974 Brands Hatch Race of Champions.

Top left, above left and above right: three Ferrari's in the 1981 Le Mans. Although the factory has not been directly involved in the race for some years, concessionaires and privateers have continued to take the Italian cars to France. Both Pozzi and the North American Racing Team have entered the 512BB and, although success has not always come their way, the cars have put up reasonable performances. Top right: (above) a 246F1 at the 1960 Monaco Grand Prix and (below) a beautifully prepared 225. Right: Gilles Villeneuve at the 1981 Monaco Grand Prix. Facing page: Villeneuve's 126C2 at the 1982 South African Grand Prix.

Top left and bottom left: a pristine 250GT Spyder. Top centre: an immaculate 365BB whose 12 cylinder boxer engine has a capacity of 4.4 litres and produces 380 bhp at 7,500 rpm. Top: the seating arrangements of the luxurious 365GTB4, more commonly known as the Daytona. It had a long production run of some 1,300 vehicles turned out between 1968 and 1973 and is one of the legendary Ferraris. Above: the cover for the rear-mounted transverse engine of the 308GTB. Left: the 250GT Spyder California. Above left: the 246GT in the early days was not exactly a well put-together car, but by dint of hard work on the part of their owners most models around today are of concours standard.

Facing page and below: the 206SP, whose ancestry can be dated back to Vittorio Jano's design of the 65 degree four cam V6 F2 of 1956. Top: the 246GT, whose V6 2.4 litre engine was produced in the FIAT factory. Above and left: the model called the Modulo. This was undoubtedly the wildest design ever executed on a Ferrari chassis. Though impractical for road use, the car shows the genius of the Pininfarina designers.

In the factory at Modena. Top left: the assembly line with 512BBi cars awaiting wheels and other equipment before proceeding to the shop floor, where (top right) the cars are cleaned and polished. Above right: the assembly line for 308GTB/GTS fuel injection cars. Above: the assembly line for the 308 series. Right: the assembly of the gearboxes for the V8 engines. Both the 308 and Mondial 8 have 5-speed all synchromesh and reverse gears.

The yellow vehicle shown here is the 512S Speciale, a styling exercise by Pininfarina based on the 512 chassis. This design appeared at the Turin Show in November 1969. It had long, rising fenders and the windshield, with a slope of 78 degrees, was built to lift forward in one piece allowing driver entry and exit. The white vehicle, with its interior shown (bottom left) is the Modulo. Overleaf: the berlinetta boxer 512, one of the world's greatest sportscars.

Left: the smooth, flowing lines of the 308GTBi. Bottom: the low-slung, racy outline of the 308GTSi. Below and facing page: the 512BBi, which was called by some the flagship of the Ferrari fleet and by others Ferrari's Macho Missile. The 12 cylinder horizontally opposed engine has a capacity of 4,943cc and lies longitudinally behind the driver. The 512BBi is hardly in keeping with grand touring, as the amount of space available for luggage is minimal.

CADILLAC

It is hard to choose the ultimate Cadillac. The company has, after all, been in business since 1902, and has manufactured everything from a 1.6 litre (98.2 ci) single-cylinder runabout to a series of V16s, via in-line fours, V8s, and V12s.

For sheer magnificence, the V16s are hard to beat. Introduced in December 1929 with a 7406 cc (452 ci) displacement, a number were sold with roadster bodies which look rather odd to European eyes – two seats and a huge trunk which concealed a dickey, or 'rumble seat' – and such delightful excesses as not two, but three beautifully finished external hinges for the rearward-opening doors, and matching trunks which really were trunks, complete with trunk-handles and fastening clips to hold them to the luggage rack. The big sedan bodies were cathedral-like in their dignity (and size!), and the dual-cowl phaetons were as elegant as anything on the road. Unlike many European super-luxury cars, most Cadillacs were sold with factory bodies, rather than as bare chassis.

Few manufacturers have offered a V12 as a second string – few enough have offered them as a flagship – but that is exactly what Cadillac did with the Series 370, introduced at 6030 cc (368 ci) in 1931; the V8 layout, introduced in 1915 and still in use today for the flagship models, was the 'cooking' engine from 1929 to 1940, when the V16 finally died. The V12s are often every bit as attractive as the V16s, which is also what the buyers thought at the time; they cut deeply into the sales of the bigger car in the depression years.

The original 1915 V8 was very much a car of its time, apart from the extremely impressive engine, which was the first mass-produced V8. Thereafter, between-wars V8 styling was very variable indeed, with the best-looking cars the equal of any, anywhere, and the worst as ordinary as any 'grey porridge'. Surprisingly, a number of very good-looking Cadillacs were not Cadillacs at all: they were La Salles, introduced in 1927 as a lower-cost extension to the Cadillac line and phased out in 1940.

After the war, Cadillac standardised on the V8 (which eventually grew to 500 ci, 8.2 litres) and let the stylists have a free hand. The late 1940s and early 1950s saw the kind of styling which now epitomises the period, with the Coupe de Ville almost foreshadowing the 'low riders' of two and three decades later, but as the 1950s progressed, the hand of the stylist became more and more obvious. As early as 1955 there were overtones of the bullet (or breast) motif which was to reach its peak in 1959, and more than a hint of the fins which would become unbelievable in the same year. From 1955 to 1959 the breast-and-fin approach became more and more exaggerated, until it finally degenerated into parody; looking at the 1959 Eldorado Biarritz, one is tempted to ask if 'Biarritz' was actually a typing error for 'bizarre'. After that high-point, styling gradually became more conservative again, until by the end of the 1960s and through most of the 1970s Cadillacs were big, well-executed, and really rather ordinary.

There was something of a resurgence in styling, though this time in rather better taste, in the late 1970s and early 1980s with the handsome Seville, though sadly the junior stylists were again unable to resist over-egging the pudding, the quilted padding and other excesses crept in by the mid-1980s. Then there was the Cimarron, a small, four-cylinder, front-wheel-drive car which excited as much antagonism from Cadillac purists as the 924 did from Porsche purists, but it is (one hopes) merely a passing fad; it is a pleasant little car, but it is not a Cadillac.

Despite their impressive size, Cadillacs have always been designed to be easy to drive. They adopted electric starting in 1912, and they took up Oldsmobile's HydraMatic transmission only a year after Oldsmobile brought it out in 1940. That they have always been luxurious is also beyond dispute, although it is really only the pre-war cars which invite comparison with firms like Rolls-Royce, Daimler, Isotta-Fraschini, Delage and Delahaye. Since then, American luxury has headed in the direction of ostentation, while European luxury has generally tended towards understatement, though there have been exeptions such as Monteverdi and arguably Lagonda. Even so, the observation which was made at the beginning still holds: it is hard to choose the ultimate Cadillac. In a way, there is a lot to be said for the Biarritz...

▲ 1989 Cadillac 60 Special

▼ 1989 Cadillac Allante

This 1924 V-63 five passenger coupé has a body by Fisher. Incorporated in the closed body refinements are a ventilating windshield, a big sun visor and some trunk space. As yet front bumpers were not standard, though this vehicle has the optional spare rim and tyre. Beneath the surface lies the smoothness of the 90-degree crankshaft and the stopping power of the marque's first four-wheel brakes.

These pages: the ultimate in V16s. A 1930 Model-452 Fleetwood two-passenger convertible coupé with the Madam-X type slightly slanted vee-windshield, and the sweep-panel two-toning pioneered by LeBaron's Ralph Roberts. All the 'Classic' equipment is present – six wire wheels, dual sidemounts in canvas covers, twin spot lamps, dual trumpet horns and a big rear trunk.

Top left and top right: a 1913 four-cylinder Cadillac and (top centre) the equivalent 1911 model. Many differences in trim and equipment are visible between the two cars. Remaining pictures: the stylish Series-370 Twelve in its Fleetwood All-Weather Phaeton form, complete with wire wheels and sidemounts with covers and mirrors.

These pages: a Series 345 LaSalle Fleetwood roadster of 1930. Maybe it's too close to a Cadillac with 340 cubic inches of V8 under the bonnet against the senior make's 355, an output only slightly inferior, and a wheelbase just six inches shorter. Visible are the cowl louvres which distinguish Fleetwood coachwork from the cheaper Fishers.

The American custom body era was over by 1940. This vehicle is one of only three long-chassis Model-75 V8s of the 1940 model run supplied to custom coachbuilders, in this case Brunn of Buffalo. The cowl is stock Cadillac, but the rest is true custom.

Below centre: the vast 1947 Model-75 on the 136-inch wheelbase has been modified by Derham into a formal sedan by the deletion of the rear quarterlights and the addition of landau irons and a fabric top. Remaining pictures: the 1947 Model-62 convertible, which is little different from the 1942 version.

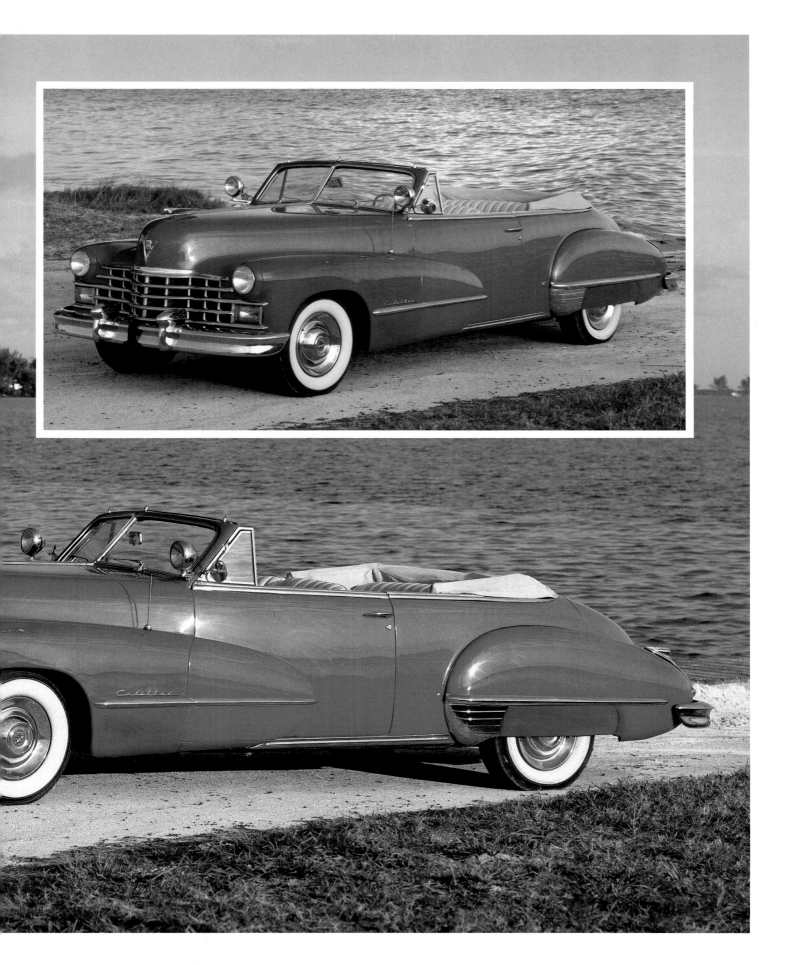

Below and bottom: the 1950 Coupé de Ville with valve-in-head engine is one of two Cadillacs raced that year at Le Mans by Briggs Cunningham; it placed tenth at an average speed of 81.54mph. Running boards and three-window styling survive on the 1941 Model-67 sedan (far right), but both had disappeared by 1950 when the Model-62 sedan (right) was produced.

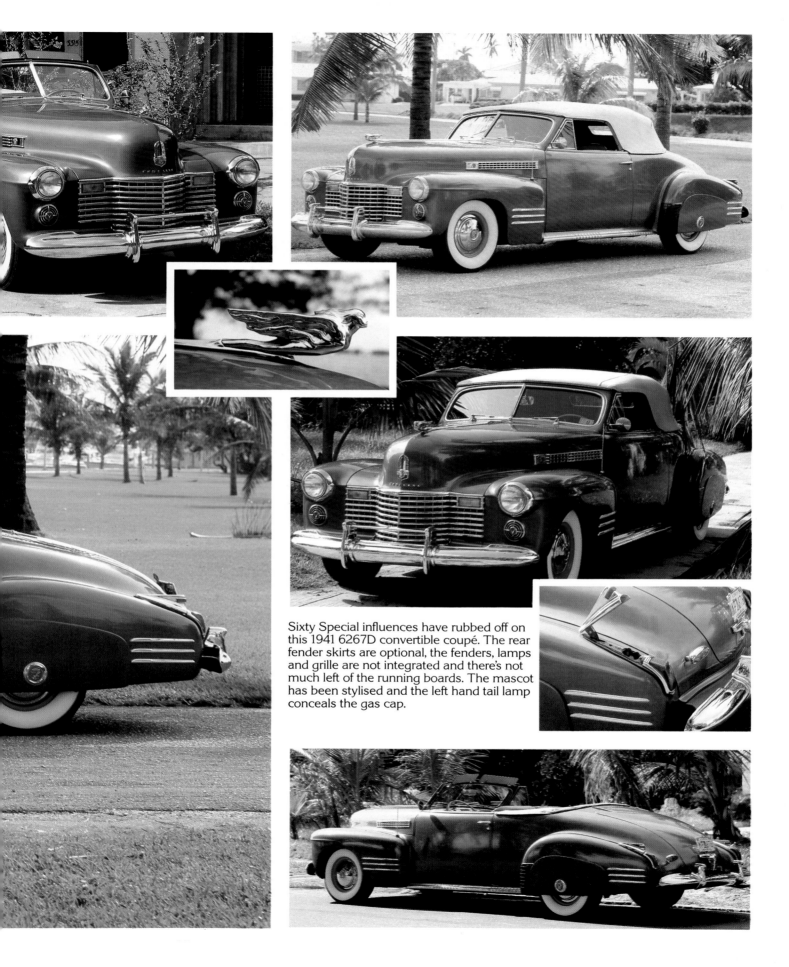

Sixty Special influences have rubbed off on this 1941 6267D convertible coupé. The rear fender skirts are optional, the fenders, lamps and grille are not integrated and there's not much left of the running boards. The mascot has been stylised and the left hand tail lamp conceals the gas cap.

A world war separates the 1948 62 (right) from the 1941 Sixty Special (remaining pictures). Styling has moved on apace and the later car features slab sides and a curved windscreen, while the famous fins make their first, tentative appearance.

The supercar of 1957 was the Eldorado Brougham, with air suspension, which cost $13,074, compared with $6,648 for the exotic Eldorado Biarritz convertible and $4,713 for a 62 sedan. Styling was four-door pillarless hardtop with a brushed stainless steel roof, which shows up well in these pictures. Detail was most elaborate, as witness the big glovebox, which came complete with six magnetised tumblers and a cigarette case, on the facia (left) and the smoker's companion (centre left). Note also the growth of the tail fins.

With the windows up, the 1957 Eldorado Brougham presents a conventional sedan appearance belied by the doors-open interior view (left) showing one of no less than 45 catalogued trim options. Two cigar lighters, all transistor AM radio with automatic antenna, and tinted windows were all standard equipment. The exuberant treatment of the fins and tail lights can be clearly seen (top centre). Other equipment included automatic door locks, electrically-operated trunk lid, quadruple horns and a six-way power front seat with built-in memory. The air bag suspension, alas, had its problems and Cadillac lost money on each one of the 704 Broughams they built.

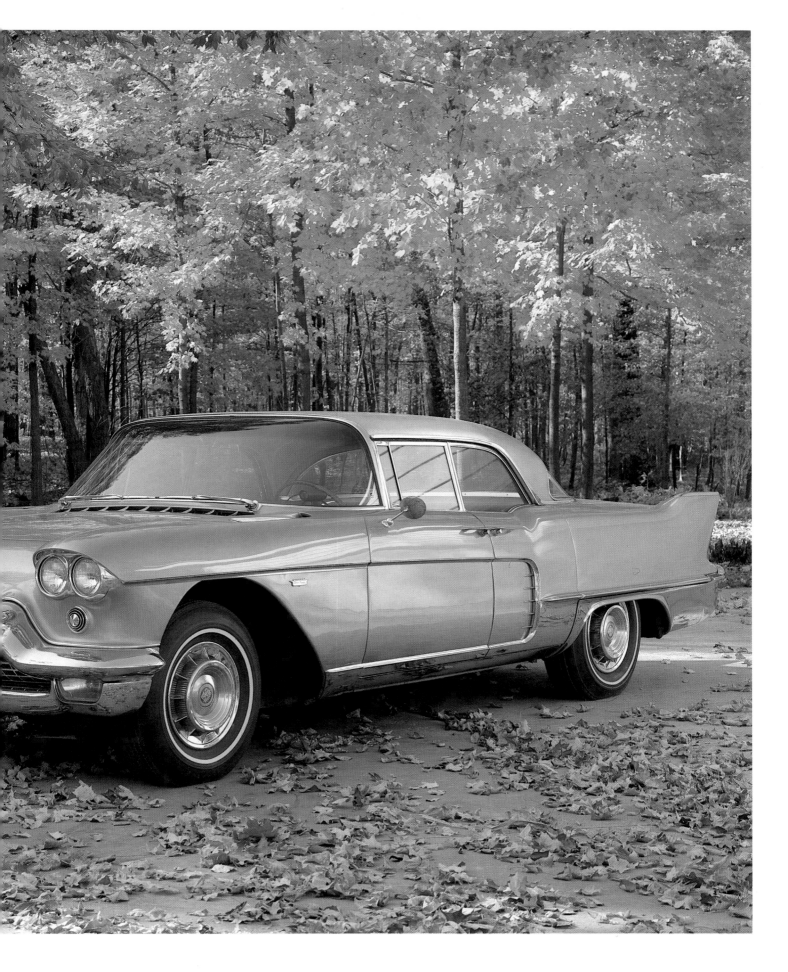

The outrageous tail fin and rear light treatment was reaching its ultimate in the 1959 Eldorado Biarritz convertible. The 390 cubic inch valve-in-head V8 managed to put out 345 horsepower thanks to triple two-barrel carburettors. Quad headlamps were standard by now, as were nearly all extras other than air conditioning. Convertibles were still good business, too: Cadillac sold 1,320 of this model, despite its $7,400 price tag. The Eldorado script aft of the front wheel arch was a quick recognition feature.

Gasoline was still cheap, congestion problems unknown and seat belts confined to the catalogues' small print when the 1959 Cadillac 62 series was built. The convertible (above, above left, left and far left) was one of an impressive 11,130 to leave the factory. Below and bottom: the smart Coupé de Ville version.

The easiest way to tell the cheaper 62 convertible from the Biarritz is the full length rubbing strip. The 62 had only a single quadrajet carburettor on its 390 cubic inch engine and power output was down slightly to 320 horsepower. Above and top: the Coupé de Ville and (right) the Sedan de Ville versions of the 62, which both featured a 130 inch wheelbase and optional power assistance for pretty well everything. The huge, sweeping fins were matched by an equally aggressive grille and there was also a mini-grille at the rear.

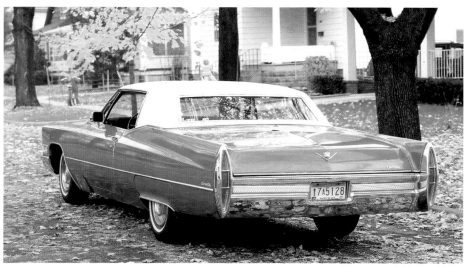

In 1968, Cadillac's de Ville convertible still used a conventional rear-wheel drive chassis of 129½ inch wheelbase, though this dimension was just about the only one that wasn't on the up. Between '67 and '68 the cars acquired an extra 6½ inches of hood, while piston displacement rose from 429 to 472 cubic inches. Integration was carried a step further by parking the windshield wipers out of sight, where they sometimes stayed thanks to snow and autumn leaves. Convertible production stayed steady at around 18,000 units a year.

The 1967 new generation Eldorado Fleetwood hardtop came a year behind the Olds Toronado and was built on similar principles. Oldsmobile, however, did not include such refinements as variable ratio power steering and automatic level control. Though the new Cadillac shared its body with the Olds and Buick's Riviera, it was still every inch a Cadillac. An impressive hood meant more than compact dimensions, so a short wheelbase did not make for a much smaller car.

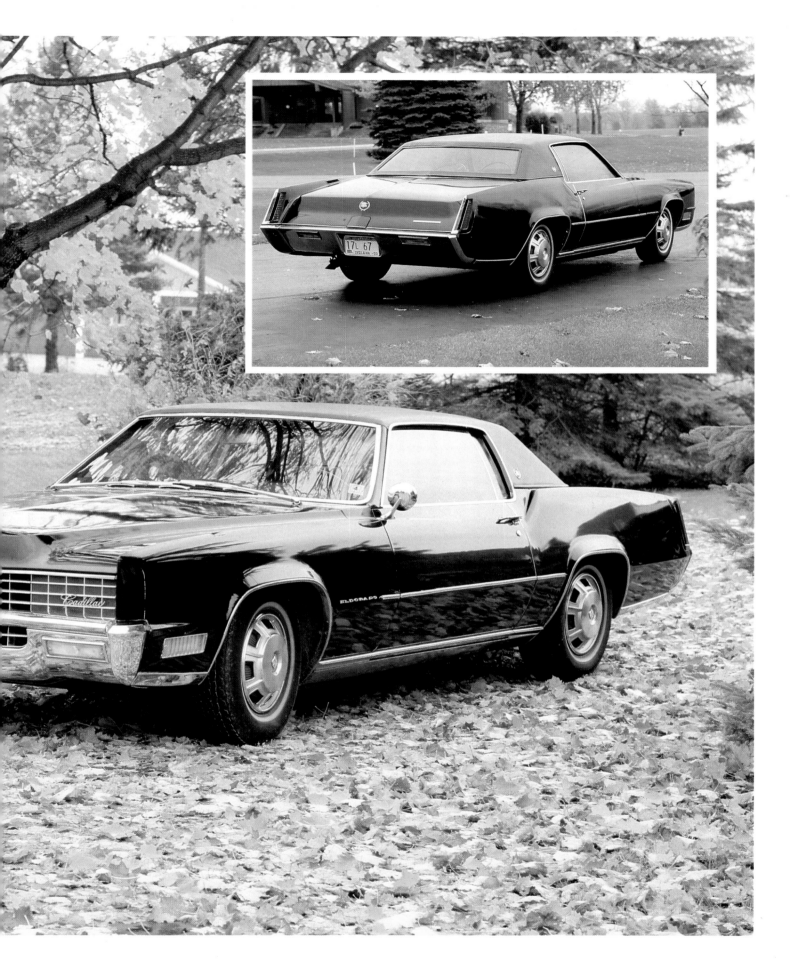

Right: one of just 200 'limited edition' Eldorado convertibles produced in 1966 which were thought to mark the end of the ragtop era. Inset top right: the 1977 Fleetwood Eldorado, one of the last truly large Cadillacs. Below and bottom: a 1979 Seville which, when it appeared in 1975, marked a return to compact proportions with a wheelbase of 114 inches. Below centre: the 1971 second generation Eldorado, which was destined to be the basis for all Cadillac's remaining convertibles. A massive look is imparted by the energy-absorbing bumpers and the coffin-nose hood on this 222-inch-long model.

This 1981 Eldorado Biarritz coupé rests on the Seville's short wheelbase and weighs under 4,000 pounds. Apart from the change in size, the big news here was Cadillac's 'modulated displacement' engine, which automatically sets itself to run on four, six or eight cylinders according to road conditions. It is still a large engine at 368 cubic inches, and in 1982 its use was restricted to the 75 limousine.

These pages: the full-size Fleetwood Brougham of 1981, which was fitted with the 368 cubic inch modulated-displacement engine. Though derived from the original 1975 Seville, the car almost had a Mercedes look about it. On such large Cadillacs, rear wheel drive and ladder-type frames were retained and engine options included not only the usual V8 diesel, but also a 252 cubic inch V6.

'Cimarron by Cadillac' (these pages) was never referred to in press releases as the Cadillac Cimarron. From the Cadillac standpoint it combined just about every heresy in the book, being a small car with four cylinder transverse engine driving the front wheels and close affinities with parallel Chevrolets. It was also the Division's first four since the demise of the Thirty in 1914, and the first Cadillac in nearly 30 years with manual transmission. At least the grille was Cadillac.

These pages: the 1983 Cimarron. The shape is little changed, but the latest fuel injected four-cylinder engine has been enlarged to 122 cubic inches, the manual transmission option has five forward gears instead of four and regular equipment now includes rectangular foglamps under the front bumper and alloy wheels. But it's still another J-car with close relatives carrying lesser badges at home and an assortment of foreign ones abroad.

▲ Rolls-Royce Silver Spur II

▼ Rolls-Royce Corniche III

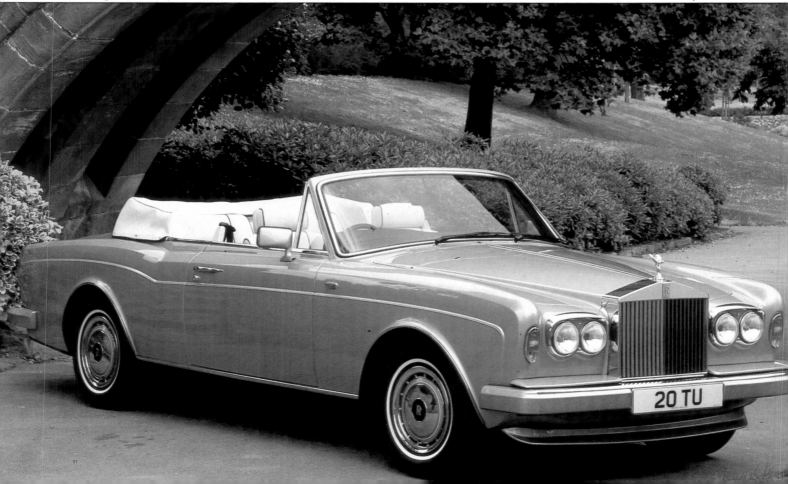

ROLLS ROYCE

'The best car in the world' resulted from the unlikely partnership of a perfectionist practical engineer from the Midlands, and the daredevil third son of Lord Llangattock. The Honourable Charles Stewart Rolls, automobilist, racing driver and aviator, was impressed with the motor-cars designed by Frederick Henry Royce: in December 1904, the two men agreed to hyphenate their surnames as a trade-mark, and in March 1906 Rolls-Royce Ltd was registered as a company.

Since then, the Rolls-Royce has become as much a legend as a means of transport. The famous Silver Ghost, with its aluminium-finished coachwork and silver-plated brightwork; the 'baby' Rolls-Royce Twenty; the mighty Phantoms; the 20/25; the Wraith, and its post-war successor the Silver Wraith, the Silver Dawn, the first Rolls-Royce to be supplied with a standard body, instead of in chassis form; the Silver Cloud; the Silver Shadow; the Corniche; the Camargue; and the Silver Spur. Even the engines are legendary: the great straight-sixes of seven litres-plus (over 427 ci), the V12 of the 1936 Phantom III, and the current V8 with its rated horse-power of 'sufficient'.

There are as many apocryphal stories as true ones about the Rolls-Royce, but some of the true ones are stranger than the apocrypha. For example, the original Silver Ghost really did run from London to Edinburgh using only top gear in 1911, and the famous 15,000 mile reliability run really did take place in 1907, in the same car; the total cost of parts to restore it to as-new specification afterwards was £2 2s 7d (£2.13 in modern money, or about $10 at the exchange rate in 1907). Again, the Phantom IV really is only available to special order for royalty and heads of state, and its engine is a massive straight-eight used in no other car. The Phantom V and VI (the current model) have the standard V8.

On the other hand, there is no truth in the rumour that Rolls-Royce maintain large, covered vans in which dirty Rolls-Royces are spirited away to be washed, regardless of their owners' wishes; and the enduring story of the man who telephoned about the bill for an axle failure which had been repaired the previous year, only to be told, 'Rolls-Royces do not break axles', has so far proved impossible to authenticate. But there really is a special school for chauffeurs whose employers require them to drive Rolls-Royces, and Indian Maharajahs really did order their cars to the most extraordinary specifications – everything finished in gold and ivory, for example, or equipped with gun-racks and searchlights for tiger shooting at night. Their modern equivalents, the oil sheikhs, really do use Rolls-Royces for beach buggies. Devotees of Sri Bhagwan Rajneesh, the guru who founded the 'Orange People', really did give him more than three dozen Rolls-Royces.

Apart from the first few heady years, when Rolls entered Royces and then Rolls-Royces in races and time trials – and indeed won the 1906 TT – these magnificent cars have always been slightly old-fashioned, but for the very best of reasons. The Honourable Charles Stewart Rolls was killed in a flying accident in 1910, and without his flamboyant partner to egg him on, Frederick Henry Royce gave his conservatism full rein. He was determined never to adopt any mechanical feature until it was thoroughly proven. Once he had satisfied himself of its worth, he would adopt it, even if it meant paying royalties to another manufacturer. Hispano-Suiza contributed servo brakes on pre-war cars; the modern automatic gearbox is based on the General Motors HydraMatic unit; and the self-levelling suspension of the Shadow owes more than a little to Citroen.

What is it, though, that makes these cars such a legend? A cynic would reply that it was the price: charge enough for anything, and you will find a fool to buy it. A snob would say that it was because it was the *only* car in which to be seen. A self-made man might say that it showed that he had 'arrived'. A lover of fine engineering would point to the sheer quality of the machinery; a lover of luxury could point to the finish and furnishings. But all of these are only partial answers. A Rolls-Royce is more than the sum of its parts. Most people only ever ride in a Rolls-Royce at a wedding or at a funeral; but the people who own them almost always give the same answer when you ask them why they bought one. With an understatement which is almost as impressive as the vehicle itself, they reply, 'Because it's a good car'.

Facing page: (top) the original Silver Ghost and a modern Camargue coupé styled by Pininfarina of Turin and (bottom) a 1912 Hooper Limousine on the 40/50 chassis, with the high roof and vertical windscreen of the period. Top: a 1912 vehicle with a Roi de Belges body, popularised by the King of the Belgians, who was interested in motor sports, on the 40/50 Silver Ghost chassis. Above: the 1904, ten horsepower twin-cylinder car. Left: a high and handsome cabriolet on the 1911 Ghost chassis.

Below, above right and facing page top: the company's own Silver Ghost. With its aluminium-painted body and silver-plated accessories, this Barker-bodied open tourer became the inspiration for the name which is now applied to all examples of the model. Below right: a 1916 landaulette body on a Silver Ghost chassis. The tubular front bumper and cylindrical headlamps suggest an American origin. Bottom: a handsome 20 Tourer of 1926 with a body by Barker, official works coachbuilders of the time. Facing page bottom: an unusual 1911 limousine body by Lawton of Liverpool with a tulip back and six running lamps. Above: a 1931 Phantom Two Continental.

Top left: a typical Ghost tourer. Left: a 1913 Ghost with a body built by the Indian firm of Khan. Above: a modern, jury-rigged ignition coil keeps this 1912 Ghost engine running. Right: a 1918 40/50 Ghost with an Auster rear screen. Below right: an American Silver Ghost built at the Springfield factory in 1922. Below: a 1911 Silver Ghost with the low bonnet line in the sporting manner. Far left: a 1913 Ghost with a limousine body.

Facing page: (top) a 1929 two-ton tourer Phantom, which replaced the Ghost but was still known as the 40/50, and (bottom) an American car with the distinctive indented wheelnuts, white-wall tyres and cylindrical lamps. Above: a fine, Barker-bodied tourer from 1925, the last year of Silver Ghost production. Left: a sporting Ghost with a light, skiff-type body in two-seater form. This is the 1912 twin-carburettor version, based on the Alpine Eagle or Continental model. Below: a 1914 Ghost, described as a Colonial model, with Auster rear screen, rear luggage rack and both handbrake and gear-change mounted outside the bodywork.

Below and right: a 1923 Twenty. Below centre: a 1926 Twenty with a later Compton body. Bottom: a typical 1930s drophead coupé. Facing page: (top left) a 1912 Hooper Limousine on the Ghost chassis; (top right) an Alpine Eagle Silver Ghost; (centre right) a 1925 Twenty with a Barker 'doctor's coupé' body and (bottom) a 1910 Silver Ghost open tourer by Barker. Overleaf: a Phantom I tourer made for the the Nawab of Hyderabad.

Facing page: (top) a 1923 Barker-bodied tourer on the Twenty chassis with a splendid bulb-horn on the offside running board and (bottom) a 1914 Silver Ghost four-seat tourer. The sporting windscreen, built-out wire wheels and herringbone-pattern tyres give an authentic air. Left: an imposing Phantom I in sedanca form. The Phantom I had the advantages of front brakes, helped by a servo-system, and a detachable head on its six cylinders. Below: a 1934 Phantom II sedanca. Bottom: a Twenty four-seat tourer with rear Auster screen and rear half-tonneau.

Left: a 1928 Phantom I saloon. Above: an Anglo-American Phantom II of 1929 with a body originally built by Park Ward, but reworked by Brewster in 1932. Right: a sporting Phantom. Below right: a three-door coupé Phantom I. Bottom right: a 1911 Silver Ghost limousine. Below: a barrel-sided tourer with bodywork by Barker. Bottom left: a 1938 Hooper-bodied Phantom III, licence plate EUU 2, with formal, four-door saloon coachwork beside an earlier Phantom. Below left: a drophead coupé body built on a 25/30 chassis by the Belgian coach-builder Vanden Plas. Overleaf: an American Phantom cabriolet.

Top: a Silver Ghost tourer with sidewings to the windscreen and an Auster screen. Facing page top: a 1927 Phantom I with Sedanca-de-ville bodywork. Facing page bottom: a 1913 Ghost with cantilever springs. Right: a four-door, fourlight Wraith saloon of 1938. Above: a Thrupp & Maberly sedanca body on a Phantom II chassis with individual running boards, or steps. Above right: a handsome Phantom II drophead coupé bodied by H.J. Mulliner with wheel discs and unusual body colour.

Above: a 1930 Thrupp & Maberly sports cabriolet de ville Phantom II. Right and facing page bottom: Bentley, who were bought out by Rolls-Royce on their collapse in 1933, made this magnificent 6.5 litre sports car in 1930 and then ran out of money. Rolls-Royce feared these cars as competitors and bought the company to keep it out of competitors' hands. The vintage Bentleys, as opposed to the Derby Bentleys built by Rolls, are now much sought after by enthusiasts. Below: a Springfield Phantom with Brewster body and American bumpers, white sidewall tyres, Brookes rear trunk, American headlamps and cantilever springs. Facing page top: a rebodied 1926 Twenty which was fitted with this foursome drophead coupé body in the '30s style.

Above and left: the three-litre Bentley speed model produced before the takeover by Rolls-Royce. Top right: the exceptionally elegant 1933 Phantom II Continental faux-cabriolet with twin rear-mounted spare wheels. Right: an American-registered Phantom III of 1936 with unusual rear-wheel spats, shallow windscreen and whitewall tyres. Bottom right: a 1938 Phantom III with a formal Hooper limousine body with division between driver and passengers. Below: the 1952 R-Type Continental Bentley, powered by a straight six engine.

Facing page: the imposing front of a 1930s drophead coupé with four seat body and the usual impressive display of horns, driving lights and headlamps. Left: the Phantom VI, the largest of the current Rolls-Royce models, is powered by the 6,750cc V8 engine that was originally developed for the Silver Shadow II. Below: a 1931 sedanca-de-ville on the 20/25 chassis. Bottom left: a Phantom III. Bottom right: an elegant body on a Phantom, with twin side-mounts in metal holders and a collection of horns and lights on the front apron.

Left: a special-bodied Bentley from 1933, during the Rolls-Bentley period, which had its 3.5-litre engine uprated to 4.5 litres. Below left and facing page: a great classic, the V12 Phantom III of 1937. Designed to compete with the eight cylinder Hispano-Suiza and Cadillac cars, the Phantom III had a four-speed syncromesh gearbox and could manage 90 mph despite its weight of 2.5 tons. Above, below and bottom: the famous 'Blower Bentley' which, for all its reputation, never won a race. It was developed in the final days of the Bentley company and designed by Amherst Villiers who provided the supercharger. Overleaf: the luxury of the modern Rolls-Royce interior.

Top left: a Wraith produced in 1939, the year in which Rolls-Royce bought out Park Ward. Top right: a 20/25 sports saloon with body by Barker. The 20/25 was a development of the Twenty and was made between 1929 and 1936. Above and right: a sedanca-de-ville body by the French coachbuilders Fenandez and Darrin on a 20/25 chassis. Above right: a 1936 20/25 cabriolet by Offord. Facing page: (top) a four-door, six-light saloon on the 20/25 chassis; (centre left) a Silver Wraith of 1949; (centre right) a 1934 20/25 with bodywork by Connaught, and (bottom) a 1949, Hooper-bodied Silver Wraith, the company's first post-war car.

Facing page: a 1982 Silver Spur, a long wheel-base version of the Silver Spirit. Above: the Phantom VI, the most exclusive motor car in the world, with hand-built bodywork by Mulliner Park Ward. This seven-seater is 19ft 10in long and includes television, telephone, radio and cocktail cabinet. Left and below: two examples of the magnificent, sporting-style Corniche convertible. Overleaf: possibly the ultimate motor car, the Bentley Mulsanne Turbo.

SILVER SPIRIT

Acknowledgement

The publishers wish to acknowledge the assistance provided by the following in the compilation of this book:

A G Hendry
A W Smith
Alan Hanes
Alan Hodges
Alan Minchin
Andrew Bell
Auburn-Cor-Duesenberg Museum
Autocar Magazine
B R Cracknell
Ben Caskey and family
Bill Arnold
Bill Lake
Bob Edson
Brian Wagstaff
C W Hughes
Charles Coleman and 'Toni'
Curt Marketti
D Birch
David Cottingham

Delbert Fellers
Denis Winebrenner
Don Andrews
Don Ayres
Don Peterson
Dorothy and Jerry Coburn
Dr Ing h c Porsche AG
Edward Eves
Elliott Museum
Ferrari Owners' Club
Ferrari, Modena, Italy
Fred De Vault
Gary and Lori Shuman
Geoff Brooks
George Bishop
Gerald Paradise
Godfrey Eaton
Gordon Clark
Guy Salmon Ltd
Hadzera Wright
Harold Meyer
Jaguar Cars
Jim Ringberg
John Blake

John Nichols
Keith Bluemel
L Harper
Larry Riesen
Les Eveson
Lindsey Goodman
Maranello Concessionaires Ltd
Melvyn Fancy
Michael Cotton
Michael Sedgwick
Mike Butler
Mike Hayes
Mike Triboulet
Nelson Bandy
Nicky Wright
Paul Cizek
Paula Kash
Pete Kesling
Peter and Dulce Lawson
Peter Hall
Peter McCabe
Philip Speer

Picture Library Porsche
Porsche Cars Great Britain Ltd
Presseabteilung Daimler-Benz AG
Richard Carpenter
Richard Embling
Rick Carroll
Robert Rodgers
Rolls-Royce Motors Ltd
Ron Buch
Ron Lintz
Roy Bleeke
Sanderson's Auto Sales
Skip and Cathy Marketti
Steven R. Keusch
Stratford Motor Museum
The Elliott Museum
The Randinelli Family
The Riekes
Tom Lester
Tom Walker
Van Hallan – Photo-Features
Vernon Crews
Will Athawes
William Clark
Willy Khan